W9-AOL-889

RITUAL BATH

RITUAL BATH

LINDA ZISQUIT

Foreword by Rita Dove

Broken Moon Press / Seattle

Copyright © 1993 by Linda Zisquit.
Foreword copyright © 1993 by Rita Dove.

All rights reserved. No part of this book may be used or reproduced
in any way whatsoever without written permission from the
publisher, except in the case of brief quotations embodied in critical
articles and reviews. For information, please address the publisher.

Thanks to the editors of the following journals where some of these
poems appeared earlier: *Arc, Ariel* (Israel), *Clay and Pine, Dark
Horse, 5 A.M., The Hudson River Anthology, The Literary Review,
Niagara Magazine, Nimrod* Awards Issue, *Paintbrush, Ploughshares,
Poet Lore, Shirim, Stand* (UK), and *Three Rivers Poetry Journal*
Nominations Issue (nominated by William Meredith). Thanks also
to the publishers of the following anthologies where some of these
poems have appeared: "Daughter of Men" and "Sabbatical" appeared
in *Voices Within the Ark* (Avon, 1980). "Daniel Park" and "Living
in History" appeared in *City Tones* (The Hadassah Community
College, Jerusalem, Israel, 1988). "Ethics of the Fathers" and "Posit"
appeared in *Ha Yotzer* (1989). "The Ant," "Ethics of the Fathers,"
"Eve," "Istehar Returning," "Living in History," and "Summer
at War" appeared in *The Boston Review* "A Poet's Sampler"
(selected and introduced by Robert Creeley, 1993).

Printed in the United States of America.

ISBN 0-913089-29-x
Library of Congress Catalog Card Number 92-72434

Cover image, *Nevo, 1985,* copyright © 1985 by Larry Abramson.
Used by permission of the Israel Museum, Jerusalem.
Author photo copyright © 1991 by Debbi Cooper.
Used by permission.

Project editor: John Ellison
Proofreaders: Paula Ladenburg and Lesley Link

Broken Moon Press
Post Office Box 24585
Seattle, Washington 98124-0585 USA

for Donald
and for Daria, Yael, Tamar, Udi, and David

CONTENTS

FOREWORD

As a born-and-bred American who chose to emigrate to Israel, Linda Zisquit stands at the crossroads to several worlds— European and Arab, American individualism and tribal law, the Jewish Diaspora and Palestine, Talmudic doctrine and capitalist enterprise. It is no wonder, then, that the poems in *Ritual Bath* reflect the richness of this multiculturalism. What is refreshing, however, is the poet's decision to apply to these complexities a rigorous lyrical sensibility.

The voices in these poems find no contradiction between faith and ardor, destiny and power. "How to open / the fist of petal, speak with a man / I never lay with, never tasting / his long lengthwise odor," the poet writes in "The Ant," an exquisite description of desire and its persistent imagination. Then, in a brilliant counterturn, the title insinuates its meaning into the poem, as this physical craving—"undoing his skin"— is compared to the ant's scavenging, a near-mechanical stripping of its booty "for the brightness beneath." All this in sixteen breathtaking lines, a blissful economy so tight, it fairly shudders.

The poems in this book are never derivative—that is, they encompass Biblical themes, never appropriating the original text but actually reentering it, so that we are experiencing firsthand the "sand and dread" of the desert ("Ethics of the Fathers"), its "wafer of unbending light" ("Morning Exercise") as well as the balm of jasmine released by sudden rain.

If the salt grip of the desert is the hard plain of truth, it does not naturally follow that water is relief. "I know I am nothing," the poet writes, watching ". . . as the sea breaks and falls" ("At the Edge"). Eve loses herself in "a man-made pool"; in "The New Dress," a modern woman steps into her bathtub and notices that "Water breaks the image"; a metal pool ("Betrayal") serves only to show the man's reflection, which is "another lie, another lie."

Images of water and cleansing, of dipping into the depths
in order to emerge changed, occur throughout. In "Green," the
opening poem, a woman boasts of pulling "men under . . . into
the green deep underside of water." The speaker in "Sabbatical"
longs to "melt in that water, return a purified bride . . . remove
the blood / that covers me everywhere." Absolution, however,
is not to be found so easily; just as a devout Jewish woman must
enter the mikvah whenever she has come in contact with any-
thing unclean (including her own menstruating body), so the
dedicated soul must continually confront its deepest doubts,
its turmoil—and instead of eschewing the dirt of humanity
must embrace it, contain it, and ultimately forgive.

In the end, the act of writing is itself a ritual bath, the
poet's never-ending endeavor, as Linda Zisquit states so elo-
quently in "Living in History," to assuage the "pillar of heat
inside these ruins."

Weighty matter, this—but Linda Zisquit has proven equal
to the task, for what has emerged under the pressure of her
unflinching gaze is a stark and astonishingly beautiful poetry.
Unlike the bland and self-serving verse so prevalent these
days, *Ritual Bath* is vital reading.

RITA DOVE

ACKNOWLEDGMENTS

Special thanks to Robert Creeley, for his generous support and abiding friendship, and to Gabriel Levin, Antoinette Dauber, and Rita Dove.

I
SUMMER AT WAR

GREEN

There is only one way to talk to you.
I've pulled men under before
into the green deep underside of water,
left them there. I've given up on myself
for these excursions into sorcery.
Into the prime of my years
I've held my neck at a certain angle
as if to say try, try to end this
clamor. All fibs and little attempts.
Knowing, as one knows waiting in a cell,
that released, the crime seeps in again,
reeling as the ceiling above
from a thin damp cot.
Bats wake, mustachioed cats
creep dark paths into tinny nights.
Under clay pots lurk slugs,
worms, life-wet vigilance. Open
your eyes, I lie, the green won't sting.

SUMMER AT WAR

1
When war broke out I was unloosed.
Whatever I believed, forgotten.
The ark that held us shattered,
leaving no links intact.
You turned to wave.
I waited for any man to knock at the door.
When I spoke of war they balked
knowing fields were fragrant
with guile. I only waited aside.

2
I let him touch my shoulder.
And I let the strap
fall. I know the winds
were spiriting through the trees
as cicadas measured the dark
but I heard and saw nothing.
I let him touch me like nothing
as though I lay on a bed of pine needles,
as though I were sprung
free of covenant, a human wish for form.
Like an ostrich that labors
flapping her wings
while leaving her eggs in the dirt
to be crushed underfoot.

3
The land is spread out
like a threshing floor,
the good wheat taken
for burning. A ladder

hangs out of night
but we don't understand
and turn away to be ambushed
in an orchard dream.

4
The walls breathe. He took
my shudders in his blunt hand,
pasted my paper soul to his
belly. We were in the soft
cup of spring, waxed as cherries
and robust for war, now gone.
His breathing begs me to lie.

5
Summer reaches its peak.
We mourn waste,
our fever mounts like little moths.

Summer is passing over us,
everyone nods in the slight breeze.
We are buried in foreign soil,
listed as missing.

Israel, 1982

EVE

Sea-mist, salt, she washes clean.
She speaks unmarked,
pulling back out of risk or failure.
She is who I wanted to be.

I cannot hide.
Once I remember facing
blood in the forehead,
on tiptoe in the brain.
I forget who I was
as if it happened yesterday,
losing myself in a pool,
a man-made pool.

THE ANT

Each morning this June
I wake in the pit of my belly.
Goldenrod, fuchsia, peonies
tightly fragrant on the inside
of my flesh. How to open
the fist of petal, speak with a man
I never lay with, never tasting
his long lengthwise odor,
undoing his skin like the ant
for the brightness beneath.
Out of these June bugs and undersounds,
I wake early before the children,
I hear the grass grow straight,
earth breaking into
curled, hard to bear,
reticent crimson flowers.

THE NEW DRESS

Unable to sleep
I step into the bath.
A small mirror leans
against the sink, its surface
a pattern of breasts, belly, hair,
bones rising through a wet
silk veil. I'll hold my breath,
watch myself loosen in the soft spray.

I remember children dressing,
someone crying, their need to leave
gathering sweat inside my robe.
I see them drift from me again,
press the nozzle close
as if its motion would fill,
trace light disappearing on my skin,
and leaves on the window
like voices.

It all comes back:
looking out,
pulled by a blade of grass,
the frame where another woman bends
hanging out wash. I'll go
to town, wind my loss into
fabric, a dress of cotton gauze.

Water breaks the image.
I start to whistle in the tub,
stroke my back with a bristle stick.
And still my face
eludes the mirror like a moon,
unreflected disc
waiting for breath above water,
wanting under, wanting to lie
on the bottom of rock and blue marina.

I am only flesh, a surface
caressed in all its folds
as if the new dress were a sign
and the crowds in tomorrow's city
so many ruffles against my skin.
Clean, I am so clean—
my skin translucent,
my body the only achievement.

SONG OF MYSELF

Eyes sprayed with shadows
I refuse to leave the house.
My skirts flare
in slow epiphanies of fire.

First break of cold,
charm is a slipper, a flannel robe.
I stir secrets, crossing myself
for a poem, a new dress,
wanting to go.
                  Nothing can stop me.
Not even the sacred texts, my calendar
of repentance.
Dashing all those quiet hours
in one slide down the banister,
one opening line, unbuttoning,

I enter my new self effortlessly.
Come quickly I call
and by the time you reach me
it is gone. Only after
                  calling it spring
I suffer.

Kiss me, make my skin light
and free! Am I pretty? Can I sing?
Ah, the language of desire,
how I perfect it, making a virtue

of divisions,
racing with myself to fall
at the first roadblock, to be loved.

WHILE THREE MEN SIT IN THE NEXT ROOM DISCUSSING THE TALMUDIC TRACTATE ON HOW TO PROVE A WOMAN ADULTEROUS

Before the poison works its fever
before the regrets
begin
and I melt in the
shadow of their presence,
I'll treat them to a taste
of sweet division
and lock the remains
in a vial
just as green.

BETRAYAL

You won't come in my extremity.
Even now the warden is pacing,
avoiding my eyes. My arm would
reach to the other side, break
itself, crawl on its thin hairs.

Chosen for your experiment?
I waited till they called my name.
Sweating under my arms for the first time,
no reward, I stepped feebly
from the room where judges judged
and lay down in a sorrow bed of straw

and summer. Gnats excited my toes.
Fires, distant autumns burned
the imagination with end and solace.
Your work, too? I lay there
spinning, the center of everything,
my spokes reaching everywhere.
As if my heart could bear the weight!
The world measured me small and pierced.

And these dark words creeping the page
like shiny beetles, insistent,
growing strong. Your hand on them, too,
crushing their song in your palm?
My soul is a metal pool, your reflection
another lie, another lie.

I'll bow out, skirting
your ropes, the stage, the crowd.
No performance in your ring, I choose
Samael the Cheater.
In his book I grow wings
and tensions fly like magnets
arresting the good air.

ETHICS OF THE FATHERS

Eat a third, drink a third,
and leave a third for anger.
And after waking rise slowly.
And after lovemaking
rise slowly. And after too much
wine rise slowly. And after
bloodletting rise slowly.
We rise slowly after silence,
taking a breath at a time.
After days bent over the garden,
slight comment about our clothes,
the dust, the daylight.
Shaking off sand and dread,
our bodies rise and learn to speak again.

MORNING EXERCISE

Distance doesn't matter. Not dreams of home
or morning filtered through a darker pane
or the timbre of his voice in every room
or blaming every cruelty on the place

or letters no longer expected, unreceived
or pigeons streaming bloodless through the sky.
Only this wafer of unbending light redeemed
a song by all the children passing by:

    So this is your home, so new, so new.
    And these are its walls, so thin, so fair.
    And this is the dance, adieu, adieu.
    And these are your eyes, not here, not there.

Distance doesn't speak. Just green leaves
push their way through a rusty screen.
Jasmine fills the porch as cactus pins
prick the palm of memory, burning in.

II
BURNING THE BRIDGES

BURNING THE BRIDGES

1

My daughter speaks in translation,
breathless stories
afraid we won't listen.
She rushes through details
like a greenhorn at the gate
hiding one last bundle
from the hard-eyed official.
Her tongue is cracked,
another useless souvenir.

2

My daughter practices strangeness,
weeping all morning.
She droops her head like a borrowed dress.
I would beat her,
tear all her young virtue into rags.

But in the quiet afternoon when she
stands next to me
begging to be wrapped in my arms
I allow her anything, even this exile
for the unraveling of her charms.

3
Pittosporum buds were blooming
all the way from the station,
their tumult of shiny stems
flailing February blossoms.
But my eyes chafed
against the landscape.

When we reached our new hill
the sun was dark,
a porcelain vase started cracking,
the children gaped, all I could
see ahead was broken and hard.

4
I have a tune that waits
at the bottom of night
when the desert stretches before me
and the window is a lens
inverted back.
It wraps me to my past
like a thread in a maze,
to a city of nighttime dresses,
shoes I can wear.

5

Breath was light with longing.
Try to loosen him, I could not
shut the window on his far-off
gait, or stop myself from tripping
on a distant dance floor.
I carried the coin he gave me,
wearing its edges. And sometimes,
he was my invention, as if the man
who controlled me was nowhere.

6

The repetition of desire
where I thought only cactus survives
comes tiptoeing through the sand,
the whitewash after summer.
Everything bleached, clothes
are hard in the wind, succulents
thicken with tongues and nails.

7

For days I gather paintings
of boats, wooden vessels
anchored at the mind's end.

I need a corner to air the musty crates,
these displaced bones
unclaimed by museum experts,
this petrified hoopoe
caged in a soundless sphere.

8
In the middle of the Judean Desert
I try on shoes,
in bags I carry them never fitting,
whistle out of control.
I think of Shelley who knew exactly how to dance,
Russians who marched to the borders of exile
with poems in their beards.
What I'd give for their perfect step!
I go on winding these half notes all night,
kicking my shoes,
flashing my sequins and costume-jeweled memory,
winking at the empty barroom chairs
that stay on clapping.

9
He never answers my letters.
Every day the children wake,
the porch air changes, the rocker
sways. Cactus flowers bloom
against the rail, against my skin
their leaves secrete a milky thickness,
the wound again.

From plant to plant I hover.
Jasmine lingers in the parapets.
Doors creak open in a dull wind.
Birds rise in swarms
then freeze in the yellow sky.
My hand on the knob
of everyone else's house
sweating for a piece of this world
that I want to imagine
whole again, or gone.

Jerusalem 1979–1987

SABBATICAL

Seven years I orbit around you
under the canopy veiled and namelessly
sprung from some unholy ground,
haunted by ill-wishers in the crowd.
You totter between two walls,
Western Prayer, words in its chink of time,
and the stark white expanse of these rooms.
I have done this to you, torn you,
bound you again.
Your friend warned me before all this,
took me drunk and weeping, washed me down:
rehearsal of immersions I would make
endlessly to dip
to be ritually cleansed of his negative truth.
I cannot be your wife
severed from roots to grow in return through you.
The language of prayer is not learned, he said.
I immerse, baruch ata, the fluid words
my body unclothed
my shining teeth and nails
my hair is separate, clean, I dip and dip
and dip for you again,
pass the woman's gaze,
melt in that water, return a purified bride,
repeating the hope to erase his ominous words,
to remove the blood
that covers me everywhere.

CORRESPONDENCE

How I wish I could talk to you now,
your body quiet as listening.
I choke on sand, lines of prayer
stick in my throat, heat pulls me
to my feet not for love
but anger I must taste the grit again,
eat the honey of a husband's dream.

Will I rise like Istehar to be pinned,
constellation crying
for her young, woman whose daughters
must cross the desert again?
Will I look down to see you flying near
whose parallel journey returns my breath?
Will I always speak to you like this
from clouds of foreshadowing pain,
marriage tent rocking in the wind?

ALIVE

In this country
if I were to love another man,
pursue him like a lion
till he fell, or spike him
with roses and cloves,
I would remember tomorrow,
my husband off to battle,
my children caught in the cross-fire.

In this country
who can pretend innocence?
Even the no man's land,
or the poppy-covered desert
where I sat aching to brush
another man's flesh with a leaf
knows landmarks, signs.

This country wears so many colors
all white and sand and shadowless,
I would travel mindless
as a river
and wash myself free of pardon.
He will return scarred.
I must carry the weapons of a natural life
multiplied, full of rust, inside.

CHOOSE

Wanting,
the enemy cast off,
wades in a dark pool outside.
Wanting, the oppressor,
grows anklets and beads
in a wet heat.
Charity, the curse in love with patriots,
gives all her possessions
to the night,
takes off her robes
and waits on the narrow bed
for ruin. The slightest cusp of wind
disturbing both of them.
Choose, the darkness calls,
choose the one that suits you.

DEAD CENTER

1

I lay on his wife's bed as he
loosened and entered.
It is a common serial, her
absence the kindest word.
And the breathing inside my dress
that he never bothered to remove
is the personal mystery,
a sound ripped off my chest
like an insect unwinged in his book.

Later the Sabbath siren
is unrelenting. I carry recipes
intact across town, prepare the soups
and melons as prescribed. For the first time
I am ready before the stars.

2

Pregnancy frees.
The egg released and caught in its museum,
the body freed from impurity
passes the ritual bathhouse
without a quiver. Red towels
for the blessing, the ones
I'd always use to cover my head,
still dripping outside.

3
Every year I read what they say of repentance,
how in a lifetime you meet another chance.
After the birth of a son
they allow your blood to soil for a week,
then you are open. But you wait longer
after a daughter, twice the time
acknowledging pain, the spell unbroken,
the life unwinged, the doubleness of sin.

LEGENDS OF THE BIBLE

Where I turn, I am uncovered.
Like labor induced by a butcher's hand,
this head of longing looms at the verge of beginning.
But my lips, my drunken tongues, soil everything.

I make images out of glass for you,
try to cut these words like jewels,
draw you towards me with their strange beauty.
But they are broken, idols in a desert sack.
Only the song unspoken rises out
of me, wild with a fragrance of flowers.

DAUGHTER OF MEN

If he does not look at her face
she will suffer, and if he dares
touch her, she will fly.

If he loves her, she will hate
his earthly ways.
There must be a book she can go to
that speaks of these things.

She alone stands distant,
the many names of God across her lips,
her cheeks wet from the mist
of the seraphim.

In this room of holy men
who can know how his eyes undress her,
how she yields to him, immodest,
how future stars explode
against her skin.

IN HEBREW THE WORD COMPASSION IS PLURAL FOR WOMB

In a room filled with cats and desert
heat, the talk is art, immoral
acts of self-creation
that fan us with scents
as tenuous as ether.

I remember wives in the market
who chanted behind my back
and carved acrostics in my palms—
"Your daughter is a sign of sons!"
Alms to Lilith, their female thief,
what did I think
she would take from me?
or promise?

When it was time I opened the doors,
loosened my garment of stone.
They circled my bed with chalk.

My body like a poem
admires itself, tries to make itself
perfect. My fingers comb the surface
for a center, my daughters
are a sign of sons,
I will be whole.

"DAYS OF AWE"

Again the lights of August dimming,
a porch scraped clean.
Jasmine lingers heavy in our hair
and in our eyes, stars pinned
low like flies in an eastern sky.
Fig trees line the street, your arms
are heavy with wine. I lower my reach
to your curved and eager body.
Night breathes around us
as we walk forgetting light, forgetting
another way of counting time.
It is the season before leaving
when change comes willing like woolens,
new clothes, this repetition of desire,
a kind of swaying before flight.

TOWARD

Dishes shine, quilt fluffed,
flowers spring with new sun.
But morning comes to waiting,
midday lull, this rage
when no one will leave me
to rummage through drawers
for another promise.
And when darkening day comes to
streets and bends I am craning my neck
for a sign, a number, some trace
of you. At night I close the books,
pull myself in to a tight column
of hope, hands at my sides
or between my thighs for warmth,
on my belly crawling.

ELUL

Welts across my chest
are a sign. I who so wantonly
clamored anarchic

against you, bare myself
repentant, resplendent
this time. Turning

toward you and blemished
in these days set aside
for a body's climb.

THIS HOUSE HOLDS

So I took it for a sign,
the way your sweater hung,
your voice small.

Sigh, and the cake of course
falls. Go, and it all
swings back, doors

slam, kettles shriek.
Take me uphill
this time, make me

jump. Some prickly
bush will leave its
fingers in my flesh.

Or slice my navel
for the gold, imprint me
to your gunmetal rope

of paradise.

DANIEL PARK

Days move through me like a train,
from city to city, street dividing street
and the need to speak is to find myself again
in the spot that seemed forever then.

Miles I walk in everyday shoes
aching to sit at last in the sunny square
where years ago we visited, ate our lunch,
rested our feet, lay back and did not care.

A BEGINNING

For three years we talked surfaces
because I was leaving and she
wouldn't hear of it. I made up
excuses: our lives a preparation,
the ritual of meat, salt
thickly rubbed into a torn side.
I was the stub, my children
appendages she couldn't hold onto.

I visit my mother in her kitchen.
The smell of ironing, of snow
are a beginning. Sunday crumbs
gather around the toaster. I see
my distorted face in its metal side,
her checkered dress is cotton,
soft and worn, stuck with pins
she collects from room to room.

POSIT

"Ten measures of beauty came down into the world;
nine were taken by Jerusalem, one by the rest of
the world."
                              Tractate Kiddushin, p. 49

"Ten parts of suffering came down into the world; nine
were taken by Jerusalem, one by the rest of the world."
                              Avot d'Rabbi Natan

Had Rachel not looked up
Jacob would not have seen her.
There would have been no water,
no winding dream,

no tribe or unrelenting
portion of sadness
dispersed on his land, his Jerusalem,
and I would not have promised

to gather them home. But Rachel
saw him and he loved her.
She was barren and she suffered
and she followed him.

So I have this heaviness
to bear. Her life before him
had also the dailiness of lives,
an hour at which she would rise and go

to the well. Then out of the blue
her future came crashing against her lids
when she looked up, those hours changed,
and I was moved to his, another well.

RECOVERY

I go expectant into light.
Elements of air perfect me
till transparent as the dead
who lose all need for pity,
moving backwards like a flower,
red petals closing at the end
of a long stem, still
upright, still giving off
fragrances, I go expectant
as summer forcing the shutters back,
the early heat enveloping and the crisp
cotton cloth spread far as a pasture
on the bed, holding promise in its
large arms and lying there
still and not still.

ISTEHAR RETURNING

> Because she kept herself aloof from sin,
> she was placed her among the seven stars
> in the constellation of the Pleiades, that
> men may never forget her.

I seem to enter the world again
from a fixed point.
Memory dust, thirty years,
learning to speak.

Flying ineffable vowels
stretch across me.
If I learn them as words
I will return

to domesticity, to bliss,
to pitchers on the morning
table, children's voices
at the brim of sound.

I watch the curtain rise
outside my window.
Breath must be of angels
straining the air.

What new thing will I touch
and call my own?
How will I know to leave them
when it's time?

III
MANDRAKE

MANDRAKE

> "And Rachel said, 'Therefore he shall lie
> with thee tonight for thy son's mandrakes.'"

1

I'll never stop paying for that slight,
letting you go as if one night
were only a night
and the years a disappearing act.
I'll never stop crying out
to call you back,
my voice a hollow stone
at the side of the road.
I gave you up easy
with my eye on gifts to come,
never dreaming an end would come
to the bartering game
or my hands could be left
man-empty, baby-reft.

2

Always this obsession
with displacement—
another's fingers on my lips,
another's darkness pouring in.

You broke through my door
in proper daylight
restless without envy.
You loved me.

I can't be warned.
Faithful to any gesture,
any kiss at the foot of the stairs,
any leg pressing mine to the gate,
I can't see an end
to fidelity.

3
I tore your favors off
in a solemn trance: looking back
I remember nothing
but fire and a form,
an animal glowing.

There was promise in the air,
all forfeit to illusion,
yet I turned from your protection
as though no chance of God endured
in our staggering camp.

Now I'll rest in a likely desert,
the only ground for silence after speech,
and watch my own guilt
rise to the surface of your eyes
that will not blink.

I shrink from your compassion
diminished,
riveted
to the metal taste of flesh,
to your forgiveness.

4
If envy gave way
to longing, to mandrakes
and handmaids, and in the night
to secret signs,
all for a rivalry;

then loss gave way to letting go
in the hope of unity,
my self a slit,
your simple life
severed by my love.

MT. ARDON

1
Just to remember the plateaus
of different stone—slate,
shale, sponge—
the climb up
to see a sphere red
against the mist,
and on the other side
of the crater
a castle dome
of cloud or rock
and conversation
pushing to the edge.

2
She said, "I couldn't sleep.
I wanted to knock at your door,
to wake you."
"I couldn't sleep," he said.
"I wanted to speak with you."

And around me, only a desert?
From an eye of a hurricane
I know where to look, when to open,
how to keep tiny particles out.

Like hours sealed in a document
not to be disclosed,
like Hagar holding herself in,
I left a trail in code
goats could trample.
Nothing gets lost in these hills,
no ink blurs from a sudden rain.

3
No matter we hardly spoke,
your final gesture holds.
In the evening I hear your arms
repeating themselves around me.

From the start I saw borders break—
my way into speech,
to cleave. Like these folds,
this tectonic shift
awaiting movement
a thousand years.
Till one day
a creature comes
and a fissure
unknown to the mountain
cracks open.

4
On edge.
On the edge of

that cliff
at the crater's
edge

or speech, a poem
pushed to the edge
or over

not life
but art.

So I climbed the sand hill.
If I slid

I pulled myself up.
When I grew silent
I offered

a hand.
And at the top—surprising
plateau—I faced
a red sun.

It was easy to talk up there,
dreams flooded back,
a stranger spoke to me

and when we climbed down
as if holding
onto each other's past

the edge backed off.

IV
RITUAL BATH

RITUAL BATH

If I could consult the Tarot deck
I would know by heart our future histories.
Or the *I Ching*
or even your well-worn books on famous lives
that must give you some pattern,
some ancient shape of me.

I don't believe in concrete forms!
I would follow a trace of the clear one,
Beruria,
who burns in me as she burned in the desert
beloved of two Talmudic men:
her learned husband
and a skeptic whose speech could pierce
her sacred vow,
filling her lips with light.

My body contains a foreign tongue,
words becoming pure
only if you open, allow me
to free the fiery syllables,
translate the dreams.

I need to give these colors
grace, a purity.
Yet last night I spoke emptying nothing,
and then bathed in your silent spring water
dipping three times.

THE TREE

You'll go back to her.
Now go. I see it in your face
when you tell me
not to gather signs.
I see it in my children
who know the sleep I force
when your child sleeps.
Midday your door unlocks.
She waits for you there,
fruit heaped, soup
steaming in adoration.
She knows my recipes.
Feverish you lie down
pulling a purple blanket
over your head,
avoiding the latticework
of dream. A yellowing
fig tree at my window
surrenders nothing. Don't be
afraid, have her again.

RENAISSANCE

Pots scrubbed,
there is no suicide!
Sun draws its pattern,
its silk on everything.
Morning lets go
softly, softly.
I love surfaces,
sky is another floor
or mirror
and everyone glitters
a little. Even the ones crying
in their cars, windows
cranked down, motors purring
in disaffection, even the ones trying
to wear covers, to go backwards
into winter and snow.
Tears and oppression
weigh less heavy
as I coax them into the street
with my perfect flesh,
my nature in love with salt,
my hair asking the wind
to part it like feathers
begging to be admired.

Kitchen stacked,
vegetable peeler tucked in its drawer,
berries whole and fresh
and no trace of death.

HIS GLORY

I speak tongues
and no one stops me.

I fall flat as the hilltop
where Herod fashioned cruelty,

mosaic floors
of jewel and light repeating

birds
that sweep the sky.

Today a plane shot up above us,
clearing the air.

Sooner or later
we all repeat each other.

Walls crumble.
His glory underfoot

bears its own fruit.
My words are hardly my own.

Because of me the birds
have nowhere to go,

the sky is precise and empty,
earth echoes with laughter and lies.

PASTORAL

A girl in a large-brimmed hat
enters the air thinking it cold,
then rolls up her sleeves.
She is stunned as stone,
warmed and reddening.
Wind rustles her hair,
his breath remembered
stirs her. How she tried
to dream his face, his posture!
till he forbade her, providing
a way. Now she's free,
imperiled as a fresh-dug field.

IN THE GARDEN

1
I am pulled to your diminishing
like a sunflower trailing upward
through the faint December sky.
Your voice in the thicket,
your weak love spurs me.

2
If I wait for you in the garden
freezing over, you'll mistake
my tremors for desire,

you'll back down,
leaving the place that knows you.
It is all mistaken

urges and tremors,
all fragrance and appeal,
dressing up to be

undressed softly, apprehended
in the dark as one who cannot
belong to such a garden,

only to be kissed and brought in.

AT THE EDGE

"You shall see the land before you,
but you shall not go there."

And as the sea breaks and falls
I know I am nothing.

I think of you pleading
to enter the land—

and only when all hope is gone,
the gavel on judgment mysteriously harsh,

can you turn outward,
give up a plan

that carried over deserts.
Only then can you look into space

and know it is full, yourself a desert,
passion gone.

And in that quiet hope erased,
self thin, want seeping out,

jealousy's craving transformed
in the words of some song,

can you open your burning mouth
and draw out the song.

LIVING IN HISTORY

You could say we started something—
a pillar of heat inside these ruins.
I'd better go home to my real life.
I'll get pregnant, grow round and shed
my hair and sleep again.
Or else I'll burn callous as a bone
tossed in the morning to the digs.
They'll find me in a thousand years.
I think I'll never see you again.
I'll bury my sailor's luck
with the ancient stars and our wild
forgiven kisses, one by one,
dreams flying out of my hair.
The punished earth where we stand
will ripen with children, stigmata,
scarlet arrows, A for anything alive.

NOTES

THE ANT

As a bud, the peony is covered with a sticky film. In order for the peony bud to blossom, an ant must lick off the film.

WHILE THREE MEN SIT IN THE NEXT ROOM DISCUSSING THE TALMUDIC TRACTATE ON HOW TO PROVE A WOMAN ADULTEROUS

According to the ancient text, a woman suspected of adultery that cannot be proved legally is to be brought by her husband to the priest for an "ordeal of jealousy." The priest takes "holy water" and mixes it into some earth from the floor of the Tabernacle. He then assures the woman that if she is innocent she will be immune to harm from the water, but warns that if guilty her "belly shall distend" from the potion and "her thigh sag." (Numbers 5:11–13)

BETRAYAL

Samael is referred to in Biblical legend as "king of the satans and angels," "the Angel of Death," "the adversary of Moses," and "Pharaoh's assistant." It is to Samael that God surrendered Job.

CORRESPONDENCE, DAUGHTER OF MEN, ISTEHAR RETURNING

These poems were loosely inspired by the Istehar legend as I first encountered it in Louis Ginzberg's classic *Legends of the Bible* (Jewish Publication Society, Philadelphia, 1956). According to the legend, after the angels fell from grace and came down to earth, they beheld the daughters of men and could not restrain their passion. One angel saw the maiden Istehar, and lost his heart to her. She promised to give herself to him if first he would teach her the "ineffable name" of God which enabled him to return to heaven. He told her the name, but before fulfilling her promise to him, she recited the name and flew to heaven. It is said that because she resisted sin, men may not forget her, and she was placed in the constellation of the Pleiades.

"DAYS OF AWE"

Refers to the High Holy Days of the Jewish calendar: Rosh Hashana, Yom Kippur (Day of Atonement), and the Days Between.

ELUL

Elul is the month in the Hebrew calendar that precedes the High Holy Days and is characterized by a spirit of repentance.

RITUAL BATH

Is a pool or bath of clear water, immersion in which renders ritually clean a person who has been ritually unclean through contact with the dead (Numbers 19) or any other defiling object, or through an unclean flux from the body (Leviticus 15) and especially a menstruant.

Beruria was the daughter of Rabbi Hananya and the wife of Rabbi Meir. She is famous in her own right as the only woman in Talmudic literature whose views on legal matters were seriously reckoned with by the scholars of her time. Many legends illustrate her moral stature. But one legend relates that she was seduced with tragic consequences, attempting to show that she was not "above female weakness."

ABOUT THE AUTHOR

Linda Stern Zisquit was born in Buffalo, New York,
and is a graduate of Tufts University, Harvard University,
and the Writing Program at the State University of New York
at Buffalo. She presently lives in Jerusalem, Israel,
where she teaches and translates.

Design by Nick Gregoric.

Text set in Stempel Garamond
using the KI/Composer and Linotronic 202N.
Typeset by Blue Fescue Typography and Design,
Seattle, Washington.

Broken Moon Press books are printed on
acid-free, recycled paper exclusively by
Malloy Lithographing, Inc.,
5411 Jackson Road,
Ann Arbor, Michigan 48106.